# COVENT

THE FRUIT, VEGETABLE AND FLOWER MARKETS

# GARDEN

# COVENT

THE FRUIT, VEGETABLE AND FLOWER MARKETS

# GARDEN

CLIVE BOURSNELL

Introduction by PETER ACKROYD

**F**

FRANCES LINCOLN LIMITED
PUBLISHERS

**For Barbara**

# CONTENTS

INTRODUCTION by Peter Ackroyd 6

PREFACE 8

THE MARKET 14

Acknowledgments 164

Map 166

Frances Lincoln Ltd
4 Torriano Mews
Torriano Avenue
London NW5 2RZ
www.franceslincoln.com

*Covent Garden*
Copyright © Frances Lincoln 2008
Introduction copyright © Peter Ackroyd
All other text copyright © Clive Boursnell
Photographs copyright © Clive Boursnell
www.marketphotos.co.uk

First Frances Lincoln edition: 2008

A catalogue record for this book is available from the British Library.

ISBN 978-0-7112-2860-3

Printed and bound in China
1 2 3 4 5 6 7 8 9

PREVIOUS PAGE George of George & Proctor, South Row.

# INTRODUCTION

Covent Garden has always been an especial place, a quarter with its own atmosphere and with its own associations. In the early 1970s it was still recognizable as the home of fruit and vegetables within the city. It was the place to which all the traders and buyers came. It was the place to which Londoners came, in search of a bargain. It offered a sanctuary of colour and brightness in the surroundings of west central London. It had a dim flavour of monumentality in the shape of the old piazza and the adjacent church of Saint Paul's. Yet it was bustling and noisy and companionable. I came there many times as a young man, drawn to the life of trade at the heart of the city. The neighbouring streets were filled with cries, and with the rumble of barrows and wagons along the uneven surfaces of the roadways.

There was a community here, too, with its own law and language. The same family would stay in the same trade for many generations. The traders knew one another. They drank with each other in the public houses of the neighbourhood, like the Essex Serpent and the Market House and the Marquis of Anglesey. The local people knew the traders, too, and would pass the time of day as they walked through the market. Tramps made their way here; so did entertainers and street performers. It was a free-and-easy place, a place of camaraderie and gossip. All of these aspects are illuminated by the photographs of Clive Boursnell. He evokes the unique atmosphere of the place, redolent of the smell of the vegetables and the colour of the fruit but mingled with it also a sense of the larger city as a place of money and trade. They make a heady mixture. But the larger context is set within the stories of individuals and their relationships one with another.

That camaraderie grew out of a long history of settlement and of occupation. There are certain places in London that possess, or are possessed by, a *genius loci* or spirit of place. In the case of Covent Garden, it is of proven age. It is popularly believed that the first inkling of a market itself arose when the buildings of the piazza were erected in 1630; that it was first of all a fashionable address before it became a place of trade. But it is in fact of much greater antiquity. The area was first marked out by the Saxons as a place of trade and barter, given the name of Lundenwic or market-place of London. In the medieval period it was used as the kitchen garden of Westminster Abbey, filled with the same herbs and fruits and vegetables that were later sold in the seventeenth century. By 1670 the Earl of Bedford's estate was awarded a charter granting it status as a great market in the middle of London. By 1750 the old congregation of ramshackle sheds had been replaced by two-storey stone buildings. In 1830 the permanent market buildings, in three parallel ranges, were finally erected. Fruit was sold in the south range, vegetables in the north range. Here were asparagus from Mortlake and celery from Chelsea, onions from Deptford and turnips from Hammersmith.

It became the most famous market in England, endlessly reproduced in paintings and drawings. The first of them was created by Wenceslaus Hollar in 1647. In the early eighteenth century early morning shoppers are seen threading their way through wooden shops and open stalls. The photographs of Clive Boursnell are in direct relation to the earlier artistic tradition. Here are the porters and the traders and the flower-sellers, the barrows and the stalls, the tiny tea rooms and the public houses, all the rich motley of Covent Garden. The life has now changed. That is the unwritten law of London. Yet the buildings survive; the neighbouring houses of Henrietta Street and Russell Street are the same; the geography, if not the appearance, has been preserved.

The New Market, as it was known, flourished on this site for 140 years. Then in 1974 the business of Covent Garden was removed to Nine Elms. The world of bustling trade was gone, to be replaced by the tourist shops of the present generation. Yet the old market can still be sensed, and seen, and experienced within these photographs. The texture of that vanished world has been preserved here, together with the life of humankind that has passed across the earth and stones of the district for two thousand years. This is a permanent memorial to a way of London life that may have vanished but that will never be forgotten. In the London imagination Covent Garden will survive for ever.

PETER ACKROYD, London, 2007

# PREFACE

For the life of me I can't remember why I was there that early morning of late summer in 1968, yet the moment when I stood at the top of James Street by Long Acre is as fresh today in my mind, as it was profound for me. It was just after 5 a.m., it had been raining and I faced a little to the south-west, looking down James Street to the glass atop the Central Market building. All was backlit by a flood of sunlight, the rays passing halfway up the west side of James Street. The fruit and vegetable displays were 'all of a glisten' in that early sun.

I don't recall any sounds with that first vision. I was so taken with the scene before me, it seemed silent. The roadway was a jam of silhouetted trucks; the sun highlighted the heads of buyers and porters pushing and pulling barrows, weaving in and out from dark to light and back into dark. One pavement was in semi-gloom, the other in increasing light. The sun was casting sharp shadows on the buildings like a slightly staggered set of cards at a near-45-degree angle. Nearer the ground, the shop hoardings bounced back at me – an odd letter, part word or name. The balletic arching lamps watched over the produce, casting angular shadows, as cigar smoke caught by the sun was taken upwards.

Some thin, some portly, rocking from heel to toe, surveying the street, puffing on cigars, the salesmen watched over their goods as though they were a flock of sheep. A wave of a cigar to a porter would bring a barrow to the pavement or road and then from the back of a shop would appear boxes of oranges, apples, pears, cauliflower, beans, carrots still with their green hats on, sacks of onions, potatoes, greens, cabbages, delicate trays of peaches, cherries, the first raspberries or early grapes.

Some of the buyers moved quickly to 'their' salesman. A few words, pointing to one box rather than another, and the deal was done. Money – mainly £1 and £5 notes in those days – passed from hand to hand and was added to an enormous bundle of notes and stuffed back into the salesman's pocket. Other buyers sauntered as though on a Sunday afternoon promenade, stopping here and there to pick up and smell a pear or apple, or feel the firmness of an aubergine or tomato, exchanging a word or two, waving to those they knew coming up or down the pavement or across the street.

Everything was on the move: the ever-changing colour of light, the kaleidoscope of shapes, the pub doors opening as a porter dropped his barrow and was in and out for a swift half before the door swung shut – all this while I stood rooted to the spot, watching, taking it in . . . Then a blast from a truck's horn, a voice from a cab window: 'Out the fuckin' way, dreamer boy.' This was Covent Garden Market and a new chapter of my life had begun.

As a youngish and rather green photographer, I began to photograph the market, working round its edges, so to speak. It wasn't long before I realized that this was not just about photography but about my relationship with my subject. Yes, on one level I was 'the detached eye', but on a much higher plane, I had a working relationship with the people of the market that became very close: that first flood of love for Covent Garden was sustained and grew as I and the market people got to know each other and I came to understand a little of how the market worked.

I was aware of the not totally unkind disregard the market people had for the likes of me. I guess I didn't help in the beginning, working with that unobtrusive, inexpensive-looking Hasselblad camera; it wasn't long either before I was equipped with my full arsenal of three cameras around my neck. It took me nine months to a year to get past my own ignorance and to be accepted, known and, when working intently, ignored. It was such a joy to me to overhear one salesman saying to another, 'He's not one of those fair-weather photographers. He can photograph me counting me money any and as many times as he likes.' All fully understood and appreciated my need to keep coming back to photograph the same thing again and again, knowing that the shots were always going to be different, unique and, I hoped, more refined. The light was never the same; as one porter shouted across to me while I was photographing sunlit wet cobblestones, 'This photography lark of yours, mate, is like painting with light, in'it, Rembrandt mate!' Rembrandt! I wish.

As time went by there were many little occasions that demonstrated the market's acceptance of me. There was the time I was kneeling in the middle of the road, photographing, when a blast from the horn of a sixteen-ton truck hit me from behind, as it were, and before I could move an inch, a passing porter bellowed to the driver, 'If he wants to be fuckin' photographing for a fuckin' half hour, you'll have to fuckin' wait.' My shot was already in the can, so I just did a couple more shots and thanked the driver for his patience. One Sunday evening before the market opened, I was photographing inside the Central Market building, but clearly visible, when I became aware of some visitors asking the beadle on duty if they might be allowed to have a look around. When they were told no, I overheard, 'Well, what's he doing in there? 'Oh, 'im,' came the reply. 'He can go anywhere he likes. I can't stop 'im.'

I greatly valued the respect we had for each other's work. The people at the market knew never to change the way they worked on my account, and if that meant I was hit by box, barrow or body because I did not move out of the way fast enough, tough! No apologies needed either way. This was especially true in the Flower Market, where the working space was so tight. However, the trucks did stop at the prospect of running me down, for which I am thankful.

I think what made my working in the market acceptable to so many was my obvious love of the place and its people, and the fact that, like them, I was there in all weathers. I just loved working in the rain; I couldn't count the number of times I had to completely strip down my wet-through Hasselblad cameras to dry them out. Even more so the rare occasions when it snowed. I got home one winter's night 'all done in', after several mornings on the trot at the market, and decided I needed to have a sleep-in the next day. Sod's law, at about four o'clock the following morning, I woke up and it was bloody snowing – what a morning! It was only later, when I returned home to see my bedclothes tightly wound in a pyramid corkscrew over a metre high (I measured it), that I realized how dramatically I had catapulted myself out of bed.

My market days would often start at 3.30 to 4 a.m. but never later than 5 a.m., when I would go to the Nag's Head for Scotch in tea with toast and dripping, on which Rosie always put lots of beef jelly.

As I needed to make a living, I had to vary my times in the market. It was rarer for me to be able to work from 10 p.m., when the big trucks came in and pitched their loads, through the night until dawn and beyond. As we started work and the market gathered pace, members of the public who had been to the opera, ballet or theatre were leaving to make their way home to bed.

I did not own a hand- or camera-mounted flash gun of sufficient power, so on the days I had to hire, say, a Metz flash for another job, I would go and work at the market following my day or evening's shoot, using the hired flashgun to get those pictures I could not achieve using just the available tungsten ambient light. For close-up pictures of people working or on the move – what I call reportage portraits – where I could, I gave time exposures so as to keep the atmosphere, combining the use of the ambient light – street lighting, truck headlights, shop and office lighting – with the flash to pick out the central subject. I would work through till 3, 4 or 5 a.m., or until all the spare battery packs were spent. Then it was home to bed, but up again in time to return the hired flash kit by 10 a.m.

An ever-increasing sense of responsibility for the life and work of the market took hold of me. Photographing it was a balancing act between what I perceived as an objective view of the market and the way I wished to interpret it. I so wanted to do it proud, to do justice to it, and I must confess that at the same time something inside me wanted the market to say, 'You've got it, Rembrandt.' It must be remembered that many market families went back several generations; many were large, poor Irish families, and jobs were handed down from father to son, mother to daughter, aunts and uncles to nieces and nephews and cousins galore. The market was still a tight-knit community; its people were related stock and felt it their long-lived right to be there.

I am aware that my passion for this project led me into a rather obsessive way of working. My mood and confidence mirrored how well I felt I had worked that day. I had either to be behind the camera, in the darkroom or looking at the work. I guiltily remember disappearing into the bowels of the market when I heard the distinctive sound of my then girlfriend's Triumph sports car prowling around the streets looking for me – oh, the dilemma, should I keep working – yes! I remain everlastingly grateful that the problem of maintaining some sort of balance between work and social life was partly solved by the wonderful Sergeant Martin, front of house Royal Opera House, who would often push me through the pit lobby door of the Royal Opera House at 7.31 for an evening of opera or ballet, seen from behind one of the side screens of the stalls circle. The Royal Opera House was to become my next subject after the market.

As I have already mentioned, I worked with Hasselblads 6 × 6cm or in 'old money' 2¼ × 2¼ inches. This was my most complete camera system at that time: three bodies, four lenses, two extension tubes, half a dozen film backs, two light meters – one a Western Euro Master v, the other a Minolta ambient/flash meter. I could shoot up to six 120mm rolls of film without having to reload. (So many times I needed a run of seven rolls!) Each camera body had a different focal length lens attached: 50mm, 80mm, 150mm, with a 250mm in the bag for the odd longer shot. So when I was photographing quick reportage, I would have all three cameras around my neck, and I became adept at instantly changing from one to another – wide angle or telephoto, then back to the 80mm, depending on how I wanted to frame my picture, for I always got the picture I wanted framed in the camera – I never cropped any picture in the dark room or on the light box. So it is with this book: with the exception of the 'bleeds', all pictures are full frame, as originally seen and shot in the camera.

The film I used was Ilford black and white, FP4 100 iso, HP5 at 200 iso, sometimes 400, and I processed the film in ID11; for the colour, Kodak EPN 100 iso, EPT tungsten 160 iso, E6 process, which Graham Nash processed, then the best lab in town. For most of the work I used the less expensive black and white, not just because I could better afford it but because it has a greater exposure latitude than colour transparency film. I often had no time to use a light meter and had to judge the exposure while adjusting the shutter speed, or F stop, or both at once, a millisecond before shooting that load of tomatoes/cherries falling off a speeding barrow or seconds-long exchange between two people.

I also did this kind of shooting in colour, but when I did I was working by the seat of my pants, as colour transparency film exposure has to be correct in the camera at the time of shooting. There is not a lot one can do after the shot is taken except clip tests, literally a bit of film cut off the roll in complete darkness and processed – normal, push a ½, push 1 stop, push 2 stops. Because of the possible variety of exposures and pictures on a roll, instructing the lab as to what time to give the film in the process could be a bit like playing Russian roulette. There were only twelve frames per roll, and doing just one clip test could destroy up to three frames. (At the time, there was no such thing as through-the-lens metering with that size of camera. Nor were 35mm cameras an option for me, as I was totally into medium format cameras – there's something proper about them. How we have changed – now there is no film, and we have amazing photoshop back-up and fantastic zoom lenses.)

My working exposure settings would be as for still life – F16 plus whatever it took time wise. For reportage, hand-held shooting F4–F11 shutter speed 1/60th second, down to 1 second for when I showed movement in the picture; however, my favourite shutter speed was 1/15th second.

My way of working with the camera had to be flexible, as it was entirely governed by the light, weather conditions, my mood and any spontaneous happening I felt worth committing to film. On arrival in the market any one of a dozen reasons might throw me from thinking I might just do some gentle still-life pictures with the camera on a tripod on to another course. This led to some manic shooting, moving rapidly between three cameras firing almost at once. This frenetic activity would cease as suddenly as it had begun, whereupon I might drift into the Nag's Head for my usual and then wander down to Farmer Tremain's lorry, parked on the Stones east side, and push my kit into the cab, which became over time my market work base. Time to relax! Lighting my clay pipe, I would stroll through the market without the camera, just looking, refocusing and again asking myself the question, 'If I had only one shot to express my sense of the market as a whole, what would I photograph?' I never could answer it.

The market had its quiet times, when I would chat to whoever, have tea at one of the stalls (I was always a tea man, as the coffee anywhere in the market was awful), or, as on one occasion, bump into Tony Snowdon and show him where to climb a fire escape so he could get his overview shot of the market. I'd just be beginning to feel tired and wondering why I bothered to get up this morning – then in a flash, like an eagle to its prey, I would focus on the way the light was hitting the whole side of a street, or sacks of onions were being tossed on to the back of a truck in a cloud of onion-skin dust. I was unstoppable, but by 10 in the morning I'd have had it and I would stagger back to the studio, carrying about forty pounds of kit.

I started to photograph the empty streets and shopfronts at weekends. The market authority gave me a key to one of their lock-up stores so that I could borrow their 15-foot-high mobile scaffolding platform, from which I was able to photograph buildings and streets with little or no camera distortion. I had the whole place to myself, weekend after weekend: no people, no cars, working quietly, calmly, with film at 100 iso at F16, in the footsteps of Walker Evans. It was a wonderful time, working from dawn till dusk, putting one picture after another into the can. Lovely days!

But, alas, there was one shocking Sunday afternoon. It was very wet, and I was on my platform at the north-west corner of the market. I had two Hasselblads on one tripod, a light stand and an umbrella over the cameras. I moved across the platform to pick up a light meter. The tower wobbled violently on the wet stones and the tripod with its two cameras toppled over on to granite cobbles 17 feet below. It made a sound I shall never forget: the sound of no hope. My world, my work, was at an end. I must have gone into shock. It was tears, uncontrollable tears. I could not move; it seemed an age before I was able to get myself down from the platform. I have no idea how I got the smashed cameras off the tripod, gathered the far-flung shattered camera parts and got them back to the studio. I never told Denis Bacon, studio owner and friend, that I took his Hasselblad from his strong room and went back to the market, moved the platform off the cobbles to safer ground and carried on photographing till dark, shaking all the while.

The following morning I took the two smashed cameras and bits to Hasselblad UK. They made the shocking pronouncement 'A complete right off' but said they would see what could be salvaged. On Wednesday they called me and announced, with some glee, that they could repair both cameras and that the lenses were hardly damaged. Tears all over again! However, for the time being, I was without camera and lenses. David Ballantine, the then manager of Samuelson's camera hire in Broadwick Street, came to the rescue: camera body and two lenses for as long as I needed and 'We'll talk about the money later'– and I'm not sure that was ever done. David, thank you: I will never forget.

Did I work on this market project for too long? Probably, yes! On the other hand, the time I spent in the market was my school, and I was acutely aware of the impending axe, which dropped in November 1974 and assigned the old Covent Garden Market to history.

When the market moved, the Covent Garden area and community, already experiencing rapid change, changed for ever. But there are those in the 'new market' at Nine Elms forty years down the line who are direct descendants of those families who lived ten to a room in Seven Dials, so poor, their labour exploited, and so thoughtlessly disregarded when no longer of use. These close communities had only each other as support; there was no one else to look out for them. Children and the elderly would go out to the streets of the market for 'the secondary article' or 'cotchel', vegetables gathered from the road and used to make their daily soup. Mothers would take in other children and lend pots and pans; a woman about to give birth might, if she was lucky, be lent sheets and towels for her confinement. It is just within living memory that bakers, having completed the baking of their own bread, would in the early hours of Christmas morning use the hot ovens to cook many a family's Christmas dinner. Families would line up along the street and wait their turn to put their pot in the oven, while others rushed back home with their cooked Christmas feast.

I remember a porter telling me that it had been his job, before going to school each morning, to empty all the piss pots from the rooms of two or three lodging houses in Seven Dials, starting just after 7 a.m. – all to be emptied, cleaned and washed up by 8.30 to avoid a clip round the ear. All this he did for sixpence a week (2½ pence in today's money).

Life in Covent Garden, except for the very few, was tough. People would steal and commit murder – it is from the Bow Street Runners of Covent Garden that our modern police force emerged. Discipline had to be maintained in the market, or else all hell would break loose; bosses could be severe and unforgiving, and unions were often involved in an uphill struggle for their members.

Listening to people talk of the 'old days', it seems strange that those hard times are held so dear. Is it something about the rhythm of their early lives, the camaraderie or the certainty of belonging and having a place within their society? For all its toughness it is remembered fondly as the world of morning-gathered strawberries and mushrooms, where cart-minders were employed to look after the horses and their loads, lady flower porters were supplied a winter and a summer shawl each year, daughters would follow mothers as pea-shellers or celery-washers, and gypsy girls and Cockney lasses would buy lavender or violets and bunch them small as they passed through the Flower Market to sell on the streets of London.

As I later searched for those from whom I could record first-hand memories of those times, I found that, sadly, in many cases I was too late. I'll not talk again to the likes of Alfie Marks from Brick Lane, but among others I did record old Rosie Bartlett from her stall in Portobello Road; she was the last to use a horse and cart. Some of the people I photographed and recorded are named in this book, others not.

I have captioned only those pictures where I can give a name or where I feel the picture will benefit. I have let all other pictures speak for themselves.

As you look at the memories this book portrays, let them rest within you. I hope that they will in some small, pleasurable way reflect the social and trading history of Covent Garden Market.

Clive Boursnell
Devon, Jena, London, December 2007–January 2008

Looking past the Tin Shed on the left, towards Russell Street.

Everyone would start off as an empties boy – it's a father and son job. Two or three years of that and then you're a staff man. The empties boy would be on the stand all the time and the porters used to carry in the boxes and he'd stack them up. Then you got your badge and there'd be pitching gangs to take the stuff in. They owed no allegiance to anyone. Empties boys and staffmen were employed by a company, a firm, or by growers.

We're the last of the outside porters now. Only about fifteen of us. There used to be three or four hundred in the old days, think nothing of working from five or six in the morning till nine at night.

The farmworkers worked really hard. Terrified of his job, one was, in case he got slung out. He was allowed to go out one day a year. When one farm boss came up the men used to turn out all the lights before he came in. Real autocrats they were. This is what it is, same as the docks. This is tradition. We remember what we went through and our fathers before us. If they walked in a couple of minutes late they'd say, 'Go and get your sleep – come back in three days' time.' One man got sacked because he took leave to get married.

I was whistling once, packing oranges, working in a cellar. And an old boy came up to me and said, 'You know what, you couldn't have done years ago.' And I said, 'Why?' 'I done that once, what you're doing now, in that same place, and the guvnor came down to me and said, "You can fuck off home. If we want a musician, we'll pay for one."'

The north-west corner of the Central Market.

Looking along the south side of the Central Market towards the Flower Market.

I've seen my father come home from carrying three-tier boxes of onions, his feet and shoulders bleeding. Within an hour he'd be back for work, looking for a 'lucky move' – say tomatoes or something, moving them from one side of the market to the other, so it's not old stock – people think it's just come in. You had to be a trickster, if you were working among them. They'd bleach walnuts to make them look new crop. Or put lemon juice over dates to make 'em look shiny. After two or three years you were up to them.

More business was done in the pubs than on the stands in the old days. The Marquis of Anglesey, in Russell Street, or the Market House, or the Nag's Head. Then there was the White Swan next to Moss Bros and the Lemon Tree near the Coliseum – you could get an excellent three-course lunch there for a shilling.

All my porters used to have a good cooked breakfast – the 'Baby's Head' was their favourite. It was an individual portion steak and kidney pudding, with a round white top like a baby's head. And there was 'Airships in the Clouds' – two sausages in mashed potatoes. We had quality food in the old days. Tea and toast used to be brought round from Louie's at four in the morning. My father used to catch the 2.15 train down from Herne Hill to the station, get a taxi to Covent Garden, and when he got there they'd say 'Good afternoon' to him, at before 3 in the morning. They thought that was already late for work.

The Tin Shed on the east side of the Central Market. (The site of the Tin Shed is now part of the Royal Opera House extension.)

A.E. Burree's on the Stones at the north-west corner of the Central Market.

You'd get up at about 3 in the morning and go to market to put your samples up ready for the buyers. Greengrocers used to come to me about 3.30 in the morning. Along the middle of the street would be all the greengrocers' vans with the horses, all lined up. Sometimes we'd go out to our growers down in Kent or Middlesex, and collect the produce, such as lettuces, or strawberries. The Vinson brothers in Kent used to grow strawberries, and put a red or black collar round the edge of the basket so you'd know which brother had grown and supplied the fruit. We'd go down early in the morning. There were my brothers, myself, the three men my father employed and my grandfather too. He was ninety when he died – and he died about sixty years ago. As a younger man he used to go to the market to buy stuff then pull it round on a barrow to small greengrocers who didn't have their own transport. That was before my father was born. And on the day that the *Princess Alice* was cut in half by a large boat at Woolwich, he was there with a barrowload of rabbits he'd brought down from the meat market to sell.

The south side of the Central Market.

Georgie Neal's grandson.

All along Long Acre was carriage shops. Where Odhams building used to be was Morgans the carriage builders. The market in those days never went further than the Floral Hall. I remember them building the tube station. In St Martin's Lane, from where the Thorn Electrical building is right up to the Shaftesbury Theatre, it used to be all harness-makers there. At the time I'm talking it was called Little St Andrew's Street and Great St Andrew's Street, not St Martin's Lane at all. Further, from Seven Dials down to High Holborn used to be bird shops, and on a building there you can still make out the name Roberts the Hatters, just fading in black paint on the wall, near the Shaftesbury, in what is now Monmouth Street, next to the French hospital.

Freddy Williams carrying empties.

LEFT AND RIGHT Under the portico
of St Paul's Church.

There used to be a lot of non-market people around in the old days – selling bootlaces or street entertainers like the Jolly Boys, and women dancing, barrel organs, weightlifters or escapologists – all of a lunchtime. There was the 'catsmeat man' in the morning. He'd castrate cats with his teeth. He was called the 'Pussy Butcher'.

A Jewish bloke sold caps for the market men outside Mendoza's, and another fellow bought miscellaneous 'lots'. He always had something to sell, and he could always get rid of it in the market and make a nice bit of money. Little fat Yiddisher bloke, a nice sort of bloke he was.

There was one little character, a well-dressed chap, who used to go round with a little notebook buying up things. One day I sold him Buckingham Palace and the *Queen Mary* and he put it all down in his book. Then he'd go along to Gerry and say, 'I've got some things to sell, would you like the *Queen Mary*?'

The Lunar Boys, they used to come five-handed with a piano and a wooden strip mat. Two of them would do a dance in the middle of James Street, with the piano set up at the side, and then one of them would go round with a hat. They had floral smocks and did the sand dance to the tune 'In a Persian Market'.

A one-legged feller used to do a one-legged jump. Five feet he'd do and land on his foot.

RIGHT At St Paul's Church.

The gas lamp man cleaning glass and
checking the gas mantles.

BELOW Mart Street, towards Flora Street
(now part of the Royal Opera House
extension).

The market on a Sunday.

LEFT The Tin Shed.
BELOW The west side of the
Central Market, towards
Henrietta Street.

My father took me to see a pony cart builder in Wandsworth when I was about fourteen. I was rather surprised because I expected to see a yard or a workshop or something, but we went in the front door, and there he was in the kitchen beating out a piece of iron in the fire, and in the backyard he had this pony cart up on a pair of trestles. He couldn't read or write, and he couldn't read a rule, and yet he could make a marvellous thing like a pony trolley all by eye, and when it was finished he'd have to load it over the wall to get it out.

When they made the first barrows it was all out of their head, by trial and error. Probably they set the first spring and wheeled it backwards and forwards till they got the correct balance. Then they found the barrows in the market would need a 2-foot wheel whereas the street barrows would want a 16-inch or 18-inch wheel so people could look down on the fruit.

One man might have ten or twelve barrows from us and one or other would pull better. Sometimes in the night they'd go and switch the barrows over – but the man would always know it'd been changed because he'd been handling the load for ten or twelve years or so. Then there'd be a fight, so important would it be to have the running of the barrow.

If it's made of ash, the wheel, it will spring back into shape if it hits a kerb, whereas iron will twist. We don't have any wheelwrights in London now. There used to be ten after the Second World War, and now there's one in Hertford, a few in Norfolk, one in Kent . . . it's a dying trade. At the moment we've got a man of eighty making the wheels. None of his family are interested in it.

You start off with an oak stock, and round that goes the spokes, then you get a rim and put it in the fire, and then put the 'tyre', as it's called, on the wheel and plunge it into water to contract it on.

The axles on the wheels are tapered at an angle, because it runs better that way. Remember, they were pulled by men – a horse can't tell you if it's not running well or needs greasing, but the porters would come in and tell you and by trial and error we'd get it right.

RIGHT The Stones on the east side of the Central Market.

LEFT, ABOVE Common horse play.
LEFT, BELOW By Grand Avenue.

I used to start at 12 midnight and go on till 9 in the morning. My work'd be lining up the country lorries that come up to the warehouses, load them up with boxes, five or six hundred boxes, bushels, half-bushels and chips . . . All in bundles of three, and sacks, which were for the cauliflowers, like big nets. I used to take in the empties from 5 to 9 in the morning, then the next empties man in the day would take them into the warehouse, then they'd be loaded on to lorries the next night to go back to the farms. That's the job of an empties boy – nearly everyone starts off in the market like that, stacking and loading.

There used to be staff men, pitching men and porters. Staff men only took stuff in, porters sorted it out from the pitchers and delivered it to shops and customers. Staff men nowadays get a standing wage. When we had a strike in 1957, the outcome was that we all became porters, except the very old men who stayed as staff men on a little retainer. I didn't want the change, it was alien to me. Staff men didn't have to go out in the rain! The basic wage was only about £7 then too. You never knew what you were going to get. The basic wage dropped and you had to do more to make it up. I started at 6 and as a staff man I used to have to stay up till 4.30 in the day.

A market porter is a very honourable profession. My grandfather was a porter in the Borough market and he married a beautiful gypsy lady who was my grandma and a bit of Yiddish crept in somewhere . . . there are fish porters, meat porters, veg porters all in my family.

RIGHT, ABOVE LEFT Freddy Williams.
RIGHT, BELOW LEFT Looking into Floral Street from Mart Street.

RIGHT The south side
of the Central Market.

RIGHT George at
Howgego's in the Tin Shed.

W.T. Jay, Sundries, Tavistock and
Burleigh Streets.

Cocquerel's Sundries, on the corner
of Wellington and Tavistock Streets.

Wellington Street, east side.

The Flower Market.

Grand Avenue, Central Market.

The Keeleys and the O'Dochertys were families that came from County Kerry in the time of the potato famine; things were very bad, in the 1840s. When the Kennedys and the Kellys went to America . . . I suppose they went up one gangplank and we went up another – we became barrow makers and they became Presidents of the United States.

They came out and settled in Seven Dials, a very poor area, as Dickens said in *Sketches from Boz*. There the immigrants lived in common lodging houses. They were near the market, so they got work there, carrying things. It was only about 1900 when barrows first came in, because before that everything was carried on the head. My father started making barrows for the street traders – that was called a costermonger's barrow. We were the only family that's ever made every type – the double raved barrow for the market and the four-wheeled standing trolley for the street traders. The 'rave' is the wooden slat that goes round the edge of the barrow to keep the fruit on. It's a term used by gypsy caravan builders, or wheelwrights, etc.

It was called a costermonger's barrow because the first type of apples sold in the market was a costard or custard apple, a little bit of an improvement on the crab apple – because in those days there were no such things for sale as Cox's Pippins or Granny Smiths or anything like that. And just as you have a fishmonger, so you had a costermonger who sold the apples.

Major Bros, on the west side of James Street, by Covent Garden tube station.

A café on Wellington Street.

My grandfather started in the original yard, Colman's Yard in Nottingham Court, where cows were kept and fed with the pea shells off the ladies on Baileys' stand. My father, William O'Docherty, married one of his daughters, Catherine, and he also ran a large horse transport business, with fifty horses and wagons, for the market. He tried to build up the barrow business and he also specialized in moving the big scenery from the West End theatres. Then he went in the army and like a lot of other people he was gassed, and when he came out his health wasn't good enough to keep up the horse-drawn business so he decided, about 1916 or 1917, to give up the horses and cars and start with the barrows in a hire business. He made and hired barrows for all the street markets all over London – Camden Town, Portobello, Petticoat Lane.

My father's father, James O'Docherty, was a horse dealer and built horse vehicles too. There's a relationship between the barrow and the gypsy vehicle – the cut-out shaves and carvings, like Duntons of Reading, they also used a draw-knife too, and in barge building too. When the first barrows were built, jobbing wheelwrights who'd worked on caravans or barges came in and probably from that my grandfather said, 'Let's make the barrow and put a certain type of spring, or let's shave it.' When you look at a barrow today it's not painted but the shaves used to be picked out in reds and blues and greens before.

A tea room on Tavistock Street.

Looking south by the Tin Shed on the east side of the Central Market.

Grand Avenue, Central Market.

J.J. Blackburn & Co., on Wellington Street.

The west side of James Street, looking towards
the Central Market.

The Flower Market during the 'winter of discontent', 1974, when widespread strikes necessitated frequent power cuts.

The Flower Market.

FOLLOWING PAGES
LEFT Sunset: looking over the Central
Market towards Bedford Chambers.

RIGHT Sunrise: looking over the
Central Market towards St Paul's
Cathedral.

ABOVE Dawn over the Central Market: looking over the Central Market towards St Paul's Cathedral.
BELOW The west side of the Central Market.

ABOVE The Tin Shed, with the Central Market in the background.
BELOW The Central Market from Russell Street.

The south side of the Central Market.

Sunday in Covent Garden

LEFT the north-west corner of the Central Market from Bedford Chambers.
LEFT BELOW The Tin Shed on the left and the Central Market on the right, from the Floral Hall.

RIGHT Looking from the top of James Street by Long Acre towards the Central Market.

My first recollection was being taken up on a Good Friday just for a look at the market and to have hot cross buns. When I left school, I started with my uncle. On the fruit side, my grandfather started the business. This was about 1890, the firm of Vinden and Rogers. He was a greengrocer in the early days and then went wholesale on fruit. We sold mainly English fruit, from Kent, the garden of England. My father started up the vegetable side and for the last forty years it's been nearly all vegetables. My father wasn't interested in fruit, and a lot disappeared in the war anyway. He worked here until 1954.

I started in 1935. It was vastly different in those days, still horses and carts then. In James Street there were seventeen pairs of horse vans all lined up on a Good Friday morning, with loads of cauliflowers. They would come up by goods train to Nine Elms and then be taken by horse vans to Covent Garden.

My duties at the beginning were on the fruit side, understudying Johnny Isaacs, besides my uncle. My father said, 'You'll have a job, because people won't want to come to you. They go to the old faces all the time. So you've got to build up your own clientèle who'll come to you rather than to the other fellow. All beginners get downhearted at first because everyone says, "He's just the boy." ' But eventually you draw them in. My first sale? Don't remember, probably some half-tins of plums or something like that . . .

Looking north, on the west side of the Central Market, with St Paul's Church on the left, towards the white facade of the building that was the first London home of the Dukes of Bedford and of the National Sporting Club, where the Lonsdale Belt originated. At this time it was the Fyffes Munro building.

The National Sporting Club over at Munro's, once a week on Mondays – a lot of market people used to go there. Lord Lonsdale was there a lot, he was one of the boys. A big man. One night, someone tried to nick his watch and chain. He didn't prosecute 'em, just gave 'em a real good hiding. He had yellow and black on his carriage, same as on his horses – I used to see him at Newmarket as well. Always had a couple of sporting dogs with him and used to say, 'Morning, boys!' If a man wins the Lonsdale Belt he gets a pound a week for life.

When I first went to Covent Garden you could look at the names over the doors and in four cases out of six you'd actually find someone of that name on the stand. Now you'd be lucky to find one in six.

Lots of whole families worked in the market, three or four brothers and a father was common. One of the biggest families was the Sullivans – old Bill, Billy, Teddy, Sammy and Jimmy were all porters.

Looking from the north-west corner of the Central Market towards Henrietta Street on a wet Sunday.

Looking from under the portico of St Paul's Church towards the Central Market.

If somebody died years ago and the family was hard up people used to go and make donations, There'd be wakes like they have in Ireland here too. A memorial card would be pinned up all round the neighbourhood saying so-and-so had died, and you'd go and pay your respects and leave something, and they'd write it all down. We always used to bury everyone up Kensal Green, Harrow Road cemetery, and the mourners would stop at the Halfway House on Harrow Road for a drink on the way up. 'They're going to be buried Up the Green', we used to say, to keep it short.

On the face of it it seems a simple task, but it goes very deep, talking about the market and old times.

The north side of the Central Market, looking towards King Street from Hall Yard.

The corner of Floral Street and James Street.

I was a warden during the war for five years, besides doing my work in the market. I went in when I was thirteen to help my mother and father selling fruit. Solomon was the name. The stall was on the east side near Baileys on Russell Street. They did all the pea-shelling in those days. We sold foreign fruit. Only English thing we carried was Jersey potatoes. My father used to go down to the city to a saleroom in Pudding Lane to buy it. The main fruit then was oranges. By the time the Second World War was over the market was practically closed. My brother was on munitions so I kept the work here myself. Solomons is about 120 years old, and I was the only one working then. Submarines were putting the boats down so a lot of stuff didn't arrive, that's why the market was so slow. And a lot of the men were away. We opened just a few hours a day, and some weeks we had nothing at all to sell.

Of course in those days the goods arrived by boats, and was lifted off manually in wooden cases, nearly half a hundredweight each one, with no trolleys then. It was brought on heads and backs to railway carriages, and then contractors brought it from the station right up to the market.

The backs of the buildings in King Street, seen from the north side of St Paul's Church.

The Floral Hall, where foreign fruit was sold, with studios below and the Royal Opera House behind (now all the Royal Opera House).

Until the war we went up at night, about one in the morning. My brother did it for a while, then in the war he went into the fire service and afterwards stayed in regularly, so I took over. He's dead now. When my father left in the early sixties, late fifties, I started again going up regularly – for a while Harold had been doing it, then I joined him again and did the move out of the tin market. We were up the top, right next door to Newmans, then we were reorganized out on to the Stones – out in the wet, but it was a good site, and everybody saw us.

The Tin Shed structure was built from the remains of the Old Crystal Palace, and the roof of the Floral Hall came from there too. It had a big half-circle of glass up there before.

Our favourite place to eat was the Craven Dairy. We had breakfast for a shilling, and you could have roast beef, pork, in the middle of the night, and dripping toast for a penny a slice, and a pint mug of tea for a penny or tuppence.

The Flower Market from the south side of the Central Market (now the London Transport Museum).

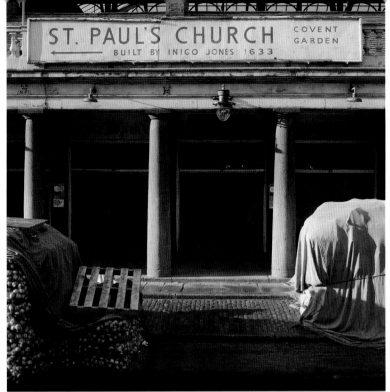

LEFT, TOP TO BOTTOM The south side of the Central Market; the Bedford coat of arms on the north side of the Central Market, bearing the motto 'Che sarà sarà'; the south side of the Central Market.

RIGHT Inigo Jones's St Paul's Church, which he described as 'the handsomest barn in England'.

LEFT ABOVE The north-west corner of the Central Market, looking towards James Street; Mart Street is on the left.
LEFT BELOW The north-east corner of the Central Market, seen from Hall Yard.

RIGHT Looking from the north-east corner of the Central Market to Floral Hall, with the Royal Opera House behind.

JAs BUTLER, *HERBALIST & SEEDSMAN, LAVENDER WATER*

NORMAN

Three of the four corner blocks of the Central Market.

FOLLOWING PAGES
ABOVE Three views of the Tin Shed: *left to right* towards the Drury Lane
Theatre; from the Russell Street side; and from Russell Street with the
Royal Opera House in the background (the Tin Shed and the Floral Hall
are now all part of the Royal Opera House).
BELOW Three views of the Floral Hall: *left to right* from Bow Street;
from the Stones; and from Hall Yard.

The corner of Russell Street and Wellington Street.

Tavistock Street.

LEFT
ABOVE LEFT Tavistock Street from Catherine Street;
ABOVE RIGHT Wellington Street, looking north;
BELOW LEFT the corner of Wellington Street and
Tavistock Street; BELOW RIGHT looking west from
James Street along Floral Street, with the White Lion
on the right.

RIGHT
ABOVE LEFT Wellington Street, looking towards the
Flower Market (on the left);
ABOVE RIGHT looking west along Long Acre,
with the tube station on the left;
BELOW looking towards Drury Lane.

James Street.

The interior of the Tin Shed.

The interior of the Central Market.

Looking under Bedford Chambers towards the James Street coffee stall beneath the Floral Hall.

The interior of the Tin Shed.

Tim White selling on the Stones.

The passing of the paper – a receipt for goods.

Alfie Marks from Brick Lane in the Nag's Head.

By Munro's, in the north-west of the Central Market.

People had a permit to buy fruit during the war and they always bought my grapefruit – best customer was the Middlesex Hospital. But the next time there was an allocation I didn't get grapefruit – it went to the Battle of Britain men instead. Iron it's got, see.

Coconuts used to come in as ballast.

When I went in the army I was in the boat with the last shipment of bananas out of Jamaica, December 1940. Everything else later was on allocation. A few oranges or something. You'd apply to the Food Office, and they'd send you an allocation card and you'd go to a shop to be supplied, depending on the size of your business, and the people who owned the firms, the wholesalers, and the importers, were all controlled and on allocation too.

All of us came in as empties boys. I remember plenty of action. I remember a snake coming out of the bananas one day because they used to come in open in those days. And scorpions I saw. I seen great coypus – great rats they are, about two foot long, and must have weighed about seventeen pounds. We used to get 17s. 6d. extra for unloading bananas because of those weirdies in it. And there used to be a fancy pet shop man who'd come round here and give us half a crown here or there for a big fat spider in a jam jar or something.

Jerry, in Mart Street.

Vic, *left,* and Fred, *right* of A.E. Burree's.

Most treacherous fruit in the world the banana. Can't freeze them, it would go black. Every firm had a banana room. Never see daylight.

When I left school I went into private service in Curzon Street, Mayfair, as a sort of commie-waiter. Used to take my trolley up to a lady on the first floor, who was a singer in New Bond Street. And one day I go up there, and I had the key. I knocked on the door, and went in, and went into the boudoir, and she was partly nude. I was so shocked I left everything there and ran home to my mother. Two hours later, a wheeler cab drew up and a fellow in a top hat and frock coat got out, and I was living then in Peabody Buildings, and all the kids came round and wanted to know what it was all about. I shall never forget it, and this man pleaded with my mother for me to come back, but I wouldn't. So I came down to Covent Garden and worked as a tea boy. Then I became a deposit boy in the Floral Hall, working alongside the auctioneer. He used to give me a kick sometimes, and I'd say 'Oh!' and up would go threepence on the article. Then I'd be a salesman and went over to the Borough market for a while, and then I came back to Covent Garden. I went into the army for a while with ENSA, in the theatrical business and came home in '47. I went with the NAAFI around the Sudan and other places, then came back here as a salesman and buyer. I'm retired now of course but I still come up here to keep myself active.

Buying at A.E. Burree's.

Mart Street, Jimmy Mole on the left.

On the Stones, east side.

LEFT Cotchel for the driver from the boss.

I remember women porters, they were well liked, everybody loved them, they were good hard-working people. My God, they used to carry boxes as high as that ceiling, wooden boxes in those days, not cardboards. They did work hard, carrying the boxes of flowers down to the horse and vans. Course, they didn't have motors in those days. Now, when I was a kid buying with my father at Covent Garden he used to get a big wooden empty flower box and pack it up tight with flowers, tie it over with string and put it on my head. I'd go from Covent Garden right down to the Temple Station with that on my head to get my ticket to Hammersmith and I'd have to ask a gentleman to help me down with the box on to the platform, wait for my train, and then ask another gentleman to lift it up on me nut again and then I'd go up the stairs and up to our shed in Queen Street. I did that as a kid of ten or twelve years of age.

Basket carrying you taught yourself. Used to keep a 'bible' – like a woman's stocking all wrapped up as a doughnut roll to put on your cap and rest the baskets on that. Before the war they used to tie a knot and rest a barrel on the back. It went round the forehead. Especially for those big barrels of apples.

BOLLAM&SON YEAR ROUND
CHRYSANTHEMUMS
BOLLAM&SON YEAR ROUND
CHRYSANTHEMUMS
BOLLAM&SON YEAR ROUND
CHRYSANTHEMUMS
FRESH Flowers
Flowers
BOLLAM&SON YEAR ROUND
CHRYSANTHEMUMS
BOLLAM&SON YEAR ROUND
CHRYSANTHEMUMS
BOLLAM&SON YEAR ROUND
CHRYSANTHEMUMS

FARRANT & REID
LIMITED

HASTINGS
29101

ABOVE Terry Irvin.

LEFT Bill Morris (facing the camera).

Ted, the beadle on the east side of the Central Market.

BELOW Mart Street.

Bobby Watts, Sam Cook's outside man.

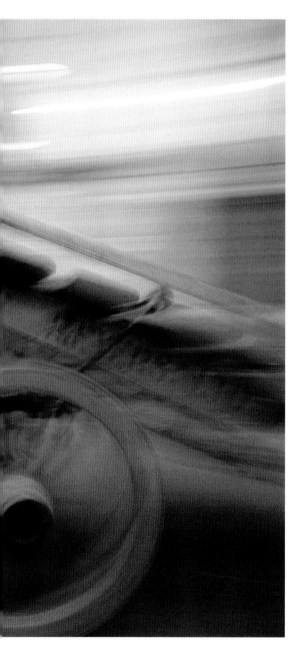

Harry Benstead from A.E. Burree's, beginning a run along James Street.

Looking down the east side of James Street towards the Central Market.

The interior of the Central Market, south side.

Buyers and sellers drinking rum and coffee at the south-west corner of the Central Market, the Jubilee Market behind them.

Tommy Spaul, porter of Mack & Edwards.

Rosie's horse from Portobello Road.

Maggie Salter (*right*).

There were some women cart-minders, like Old Nell outside the Nag's Head. The last one was Alice, down by the *News of the World*. They were your mothers – you couldn't take liberties. They also used to bring up the peas in baskets. The majority had relations in the market – sons or brothers. Swearing, that's one thing they'd give as good as they got. They'd do the shelling fast, with one hand, and broad beans. No knives, just fingers. All the old girls used to work in the pea-shelling area. They used to slice runner beans, trim broccoli for the top-class hotels, peel potatoes, or scrub the new potatoes. Baileys used to do this, though they were really commission salesmen. They used to do Fropacks – that was their trade name even before the war.

Every area of the market had its well-known visitors, like these old girls. Like Nellie Whitman – she swears like a trooper. She had her hat pulled down over her eyes, and kept a stall in Brixton market. She did the buying. If you saw a political argument she'd be in it. A real hot Tory. They used to egg her on and there'd be laughter to get her to lose her temper. But no one really lost their temper in the old market. You'd have your say and that was it. One old fellow said to me when I first came in the market selling, 'Never, never lose your temper. If you do they'll harp on it and always be egging you on.'

Nothing was wasted in the old market. In the new one, there's food on the ground and in the old one there never was. The old girls used to pick it up, for one thing. They'd take it home to the flats near by.

Sue Homewood, who grew carnations
and ran a flower shop.

Horses always found their way about, up the
street – you'd more or less come up behind, with
the cart. I woke up, going to market one night,
and found myself standing outside the horse stall
with him waiting for me to take the bit out of his
mouth for a drink! And once I followed Charlie
Tyle's van from Lewisham, and I suppose I must
have dropped off to sleep, and when we got to
Borough market he came and woke me up:
'What are you doing behind me?' he said, and I
said, 'I suppose I must have dropped off to sleep,
and my horse followed yours. How am I going to
get back?' – because I didn't know the way to
Covent Garden from there, of course . . .

One time going home I woke up with about
twenty trams behind me. The old horse knew you
see that if she pulled the van on to the tramlines,
the wheels got into the grooves and the cart didn't
need any pulling. Clever old horse. It would run
down the tramlines. I was woken up with a copper
pinching my leg outside the Green Man about 11
o'clock – 'Get off the road!' he said, and there were
twenty or thirty trams behind me, all clanging
their bells and the drivers swearing . . . at night we
used to ride on the tram lines, but you had to be
careful or the iron band would come off, if you
pulled her up too sharp and twisted the wheel.

Flower ladies.

ABOVE LEFT Mr and Mrs Mitchell at the newspaper stall by Tavistock
Chambers, between James Street and Mart Street.
BELOW LEFT Saleswoman at the potato market.
BELOW RIGHT Rosie from Portobello.

R. Mitchell's empties man.

Sales box on the Stones.

Norman of Minnear, Munday and Miner.

*Left to right* Morris Jackson, Frank Bery and Len Oades.

BELOW Rosie and horse by St Paul's Church.

RIGHT James Street.

FOLLOWING PAGES In the Central Market.

LEFT Book-keeper in South Row.

ABOVE LEFT Lewis Emanuel in his shop in James Street.
ABOVE RIGHT Inside the Tin Shed.

We used to buy cabbages by the tally or half-tally – that was a lot. There were sixty cabbages in a tally. The word comes up from the docks – you'd tally up as far as sixty and start again – it was probably as much as one man could carry. A tally of onions would be just a good armful. Then we had coir nets for produce in the old days, and pottle baskets for the loose produce.

There's a difference between the customers who come to a grower like me, and the ones who go to a commission salesman. Mine were greengrocers. Theirs were provincial greengrocers and wholesalers, wanting produce to go out to other towns like Manchester or Birmingham. Sometimes stuff goes out on lorries all the way to Carlisle. In the old days, everything for the whole country came through Covent Garden. My clients were Londoners, West End stores like Barkers of Kensington, Cousin Brothers of Marble Arch, Skinners in Elizabeth Street, or Morris of Marylebone.

LEFT Sales on the Stones.

Looking over the Central Market towards
Drury Lane, the Flower Market and, in the
distance, St Paul's Cathedral.

I was in the boys' gang when I first went to work on the farm at Sipson, 500 acres of market garden. I met my wife on the farm. We were married sixty-seven years, bless her, good girl she was, good girl.

Fourteen bob a week was what I got, even when I started as a stoker on the steam lorry, going up to Covent Garden Market five nights a week. I was fifteen and a half. A stoker was considered a boy's job and when you got to eighteen you were too old.

I'd start the fire in the steam lorry about 8 in the evening. By 10, 10.30, I'd have it all fired up with a good head of steam. My driver'd turn up and we'd hitch up the trailer. Both van and trailer would be piled high . . . About 10.30 we'd pull out of the farmyard, then set off up the Great West Road, 8mph and me shovelling coal into the fire box all the time to keep the steam pressure up.

We'd get to Covent Garden after 12.30, one o'clock in the morning. We were growers, so we sold from the Stones at the bottom of James Street, either side of the ramp . . . About four, five in the morning we'd hitch up the empties trailer and then slowly get out of Covent Garden. It was that jammed, horse and van, steam van and trailer, and petrol lorries, it might take us up to an hour to get to Leicester Square.

When I was twenty-one I got my licence to drive petrol lorries. . . . Carried on driving and selling right through the war, driving with lights so dim you couldn't see a fucking thing 'cos the black-out, and working in the market with no lighting, the black market, there was some things went on in those days I can tell you.

After the war the farm began to go downhill . . . by the 1960s it was all but gone to the airport.

LEFT Cleaner.
BELOW Feral cat.

RIGHT Scavenging pigeons

LEFT AND RIGHT Some of those who passed through the market.

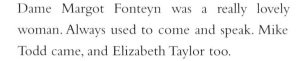

Dame Margot Fonteyn was a really lovely woman. Always used to come and speak. Mike Todd came, and Elizabeth Taylor too.

Before the war the Duke of Windsor used to come through – come for a drink. He was a good customer in the market.

Peter Finch and Dana Andrews wanted a drink at five in the morning once. Finch was no man to mess around with.

Michael Bentine had a very old Rolls, and he parked it down Drury Lane and we all got him fixed up with oranges. He had a big teddy-bear coat on, worth about £250, and we got him all lumbered up, out he went stuffed right with oranges. And round the corner came two well-known market coppers, one of them Tony Ambrose, and the buttons burst off him and all these oranges fell to his toes. 'There's Michael Bentine' – they called him back – 'We know they're for your mum!' 'We all know about your mother!' they shouted . . . the market used to be full up with the famous and the infamous.

The sights you don't see down here, well, I saw a girl come through the market early one morning. Obviously stoned out of her mind – she came from a very good family, though, you could tell that. She appeared like a six-foot, willowy figure, you know, in the funny light of the early morning, with a bright yellow long dress, a big floppy hat and a shawl, and these long boots on. And someone whistled 'These boots are made for walking', and everyone finished up whistling it, but you could have dropped a bomb and not woken her up.

I remember when Lily Langtry used to got to Rules and King Edward would visit her there. I saw him go through Seven Dials. King Edward would walk through with his aide-de-camp miles behind him – he wouldn't have them near. 'Hello! How are you!' he'd say. He was a good old soul, he was.

Marie Lloyd, Daisy James, Nellie Wallace, Harry Lauder, all used to be in the vicinity, they all came through. Up Denmark Street.

The utter congestion was the cause of the atmosphere. Tito Gobbi could walk through here one morning and say hello to you.

FOLLOWING PAGES
The Flower Market.
FROM TOP, LEFT TO RIGHT Hagglers, like Charlie Barber, seen here, would break up a box of flowers and sell them as individual bunches; Mickey Edinburgh, Coraran's boy; Peter Bullen (holding the box of carnations); customer being loaded with flowers.

Charlie Bosey of Allan & Greenwood serving one of the Sisters who regularly shopped in the market.

Women used to sell oranges to people outside Drury Lane Theatre, especially at pantomime time. I saw Dan Leno and Arthur Campbell there. And my brother used to get a job as an extra in the Opera House sometimes. We could hear them rehearsing from the street. Beautiful. I remember royalty going in, they had a private entrance by the Floral Hall. The carriages used to come right round Long Acre and down Bow Street, through the archway, which isn't used now. They were all in fancy dress, and afterwards people used to come round the market and give us money sometimes.

There used to be a jellied eel stall just outside the Floral Market, a shilling for a plate. Lou Myer – we used to call him Jelly – ran it. He would bring a plate over for my mother, stand and chat while she ate it, and bread with it, and then take the plate back for her.

Another man used to come around with a horse and cart selling block salt and carbolic – we used that to scrub the stairs down, do the washing, things like that. Red and yellow soap he carried, in big blocks. You had to keep things clean in those days, we all lived on top of each other, and families were all living one to a room. When a woman had a confinement, they borrowed all the pots off the neighbours and boiled up the water all together.

FOLLOWING PAGES
CLOCKWISE FROM TOP LEFT Buyer; porter; Sister of the Poor; Sister and Rosie; buyer; Sisters hiring a taxi to take their produce back to the convent; florist; bowler-hatted accountant.

RIGHT TOP Barrow boy.
RIGHT CENTRE AND BOTTOM
Porters with their cotchel.

OPPOSITE, TOP TO BOTTOM
'Cotchel' Rosie; cotchel;
Ronny ('Rocket') Spittle.

Rosie was with us for forty years. There are eight of us here, and she used to make eighteen cups of tea at a time – and spread them all over the market, in exchange for a coffee or something . . . she took home armfuls daily. She couldn't have eaten it all. She was fantastic. We used to say, 'We saw you stealing the guvnor's milk money,' and she'd swear back at us, 'Get off, etc., etc.' We've got a little cat here, always reminds me of Rosie, got those same eyes that seem to go right through you.

We took her to the pub one day for a drink to be friendly, and asked her what she wanted – 'A double brandy,' she said.

Old Rosie? Tough she was. Used to do coffee and cleaning for Hamiltons. She never wanted to appear growing old. As long as she could walk or crawl she'd do it. People never got sacked. Towards the end she couldn't do much except make tea and keep company but they'd never sack her, as long as she could keep the place tidy. We used to give her a few vegetables to get us coffee, sometimes. She'd never wait till it fell on the floor. She'd take the stuff off the box. If I gave her a cauli she'd say, 'I don't want that one, haven't you got a better one?'

The porters wore plain trousers and tweed waistcoats, the salesmen wore bowler hats and a stiff collar. They used to be much better dressed – more accurately dressed – in the old days. The upper classes were correctly dressed, the porters, suitably dressed, according to their station and work. Some of the porters come dressed as good as salesmen today.

LEFT Portobello Rosie by St Paul's Church.

My dad was in the market down Portobello Road. Half a crown a week I earned after school. I was seventeen when he was taken ill. I'm sixty-eight now, so I've done fifty-six years here. When my daughter Margaret was twelve she used to drive the horse to market. She didn't care, a real tomboy. She'd load the van like a bleeding man. I went up there with my dad when I was a kid. I used to have to find him in the Nag's Head with all the fellows who'd done all the buying. He kept his money in a pea bag on his back. I always had something he bought me, a box of scent, never without a silk, always bird's eye, blue and white or black and white. There's nothing I wanted for when my father was alive, nor when my husband was alive either.

I was married forty-one years, on the 12th of April. I never been used to drawing a pension, always handled money.

I've got a lot of aggravation down here now. They're all learners, aren't they? Anyone who upsets my girl Margaret I come up after them.

My horse and wagon was the last in the market. When I was in hospital I had flowers and a box of peaches delivered, and strawberries out of Monro's, everything of the best. Stallholders, nothing from them.

You remember me to all the porters there, don't be afraid. Harry the Poof, and Denny and Norman Wisdom, he works at Barkers, and Old Ernie's boy who works for Bernie's.

Lovely days. Lovely days.

RIGHT ABOVE Charlie, a salesman.
RIGHT BELOW The west side of James Street.

Rosie with her hand-picked cotchel.

Tim White (*front*), next to Billy Armon.

Very often we sold some of our best-quality stuff to the inside firms. Tuckers was a regular, and he'd sell it on to his customers. He'd do them a favour, early in the morning, by nipping down the growers like us and buying ten or twenty boxes of cauliflowers or green garden peas, fresh strawberries or raspberries . . . one thing, the commission buyers, those receiving fruit from the country, during the war they'd go round buying up all the cabbages, which weren't controlled at that time. Then you'd pay double or treble on the cabbages in order to get the apples you wanted, because they were controlled. so you'd pay 5*s.* on a box of apples and 15*s.* on the cabbages. That's how the black market worked. They did it with everything not controlled. Whatever was in short supply, they'd corner it. Some firms wouldn't sell, of course, but if they were good salesmen they'd just book it, not pay for it, wait until their customers came in, sell it, then send a porter over for it. That's just good business, no trickery. Just getting a little sales commission.

ABOVE Coffee stall by the Floral Hall.
BELOW Bill, foreman of Dennis & Cooper's, and (*right*) Tony Buckle, who became leader of the Covent Garden branch of TGWU.

A lot of trading goes on from generation to generation, you know. Fathers have bought off my father, sons off us, two or three generations, and their sons will buy off Michael. I've had customers say to me, 'I've bought strawberries off you all summer. I haven't made any money. You've been too dear for me with your price.' But they've stuck with me all through the summer. Another man might make a lot with the same price, though. Depends on their area.

Football and rugby times, we used to get the Scotsmen in their kilts coming round for a drink. Then there were the old tramps and the scroungers. There was an old boy who used to sing opera songs, beautiful old voice he had. He's been coming here on and off for ten or fifteen years. He sang from *The Gondoliers*, *Barber of Seville*, *Madam Butterfly*, all the well-known pieces. I always got a penny or two for him. I always used to search him out when I heard his songs. He used to walk up Bow Street backwards, singing as he went, right up the middle of the street.

Other street entertainers used to come right up the Tin Shed. Old organ grinders years ago would stand outside the pubs. The great thing about old Covent Garden was that it was intermingled with so much of London, from the richest to the poorest tenements, like the Peabody Buildings.

ABOVE Salesman.
BELOW Porter.

ABOVE FAR LEFT James Street.
ABOVE LEFT A sleeping toff in James Street.
ABOVE FAR RIGHT A milkman in Wellington Street.
FAR LEFT The west side of James Street.
LEFT The tobacco kiosk by Tavistock Chambers.
RIGHT Looking for directions from the beadle.

My first trip up to the market by myself, I well remember. I'd been up with other people before, but the first time the horse took me up from Lewisham to the right spot in the market. That was my first impression, this horse leading me in. I was apprehensive of course because all the porters were real Cockneys. When you first went, you were deaf and dumb, and had to follow what everyone said.

Our business was done by eight o'clock in the morning before the war – there was a greater volume of stuff then too, The latter years I remember mostly that the quality of the stuff had improved a lot. There were plenty of little old boys with horses and carts who used to buy poor-quality stuff in the old days and go around the streets, but you couldn't get rid of that stuff today. You're restricted from even offering for sale the 'secondary article' – like little frosted touches on cauliflowers. I've seen men in the old days cut out a brown bit, cut up another cauliflower and put a good piece in the hole and sell it whole. Another fellow used to dust them with powder to make them look white – those old street traders I mean. But people were sensible then. They knew if an apple had got a bruise on it, if you cook it immediately it will still be all right. Now no one wants to buy it. They've got to be the same size, the same colour. Honest, with a little bit of knowledge the waste would keep people fed.

Inside the Central Market.

When we were loading lorries, we'd hold the bottom up and someone else would stand at the top and help roll it on. You'd get 2*d*. or a shilling at one time for shifting that lot and with 30*s*. top weight as a retainer, that was your lot. A good man got £4 a week before the war, and you'd have to work long hours for that. You were paid by packages, not by weight, remember. Take a big firm – people'd come and buy the stuff and the foreman of the firm would go through his tickets at the end of the day and he'd know how much porterage he'd got and so it would be shared out and every man would know what wages he'd have to come. Nowadays men work to a basic level, even if they don't do anything, and the guvnor has to pay out that wage himself.

We used to deal in sovereigns, half-sovereigns, in gold. Only paper was for a five-pound note. You could melt it down and it was a sovereign's worth of gold. I remember my mother, 'tink, tink, tink', counting the gold and silver. Now you've got iron in your pocket. They had to call the pennies in 'cos you had more than a penny's worth of copper there, and people were melting it down. My mother used to wear a pocket to keep her money in. You didn't need to carry much, because a few sovereigns bought a lot.

By Barney Springer's (now Tuttons).

ABOVE The Flower Market.
BELOW The south side of
the Central Market.

ABOVE Wellington Street.
BELOW Bundling lavender
by the covered way.

You've got growers next to you with twice as much for half the price. Then you have to weigh up how many regular customers you've got and maybe come down in price to hold them. Prices are fixed purely by supply and demand, not by how much it cost you to grow the produce in the field. Size and continuity is what counts, because you know what you've got coming up tomorrow. A good-quality man would buy in the early morning. I'd sell the same stuff cheaper in the day to get rid of it to less particular buyers then.

Old Charlie, who's eighty-five, said the bar in the Essex hadn't changed since his father's time – he could remember Lord Rosebery in there and he'd say, 'Come on lads', and throw a few sovereigns in the air, and the lads would have a scramble. They'd kick one another, jump on each other, to get it, laughing all the time.

Old Sam, his son fetched the coffin and put it on the floor of every pub his old man used in his time, the Essex, the Market House, and all the rest. He and the bearers put it down, and the son treated the bar – like this, 'Goodbye, Sam,' they'd say, up with the coffin and on to the next. He always sat on that stool there and was he angry if anyone else was on it when he came in. In the fifties this was.

A scene from the Hitchcock film *Frenzy*, which was shot in the market. Hitchcock's father was a stallholder in Covent Garden.

There used to be a policeman controlling the trams then. There was so much traffic, with the stuff coming up from all over, Lincolnshire, Cambridgeshire, Cornwall, all over. There'd be cart-minders and horse-minders to see the horses got a nosebag on, and to move the van in case a fresh load came in to a particular place. It's only a name today, but years ago he had something to do, the cart-minder. We used to give the porters sixpence to feed the horses while we had a bit of bread and cheese, or we'd water the horses at the George at Lewisham – that was a coaching inn and so was the Green Man. It had a water trough in the old days. Or an old tramp on the road would hold the horses for you. The first time I went with one particular horse, I couldn't get past a pub. He'd been taught to stop every time he came to a pub . . . this driver used to stop at every pub till 10.30. You found out what other drivers did without being told! One used to get through twenty pints a night – and at a time when they were supposed not to get any money.

Odd characters? I remember one, a fellow who used to come around in shorts. He really was a layabout. Threw himself in the Thames. He was a lord, but he let himself go.

RIGHT AND FAR RIGHT
The Nag's Head.
BELOW LEFT The Market House.
BELOW RIGHT The Essex Serpent..

I always reckon I'm better working with a boozer than a tea man. He'd blow on the fucking tea for a fucking half hour. Whereas a boozer's straight in and out before the door swings shut, he's off.

I'm a connoisseur of Guinness. My sister sold outside Henekeys, in the Strand. When one of 'em got married, of course, living near in Drury Lane, we had the wedding party in Henekeys. In those days kids were allowed in the pubs, four-and-a-half, me, and I'm in Henekeys. Remember it as though it were yesterday, drinking everybody's beer, don't know what it was, bitter or stout. They used to sell little ha'penny sponge cakes, and father was buying them and I was dipping them in the stout and I gets drunk, I was carried out of Henekeys at four-and-a-half years of age, there you are, it's the gospel, I've used it all my life!

LEFT ABOVE AND BELOW Barney Springer's (now Tuttons).

I worked for the best man in dates once. It was a ritual – the arrival of the first load of dates at the end of November. If it had been raining and the driver arrived without pulling the canvas sheet down, he'd not get his money. It was just like the King's funeral, this lorry would come round the market, he'd lift the covers, take out a box, give you one date and say, 'How are they?' Blinding man to work for. You got a lot of money with him, but when I left and went to work next door, I popped back to borrow a broom one day and he said, 'No, you don't work here no more.' And he wouldn't use a handkerchief, he'd use the tomato papers.

People used to come down in June to get their names down on the list. Hard, he was – worse than a prison sentence. One guy sold some dates below the price he'd paid for them, and all this man said was, 'No more dates.' This guy, he'd come from up north, all the way, and he said, 'Blimey, fine me £100 or something.' But all he'd say was, 'No more dates.'

He lost a box one day. He went all round the London markets. Found 'em. I was taking twelve cartons of 72s over to J.B. Thomas one day and he said, 'Where you going, Harry?' So I told him and he said, 'Wait a minute, do you know the firm?' – only one of the biggest firms in the market! He was mean. They shut down, didn't move to the new market. Sole importer of J.L. Dates, came from Marseilles – Hochat was the name, I believe.

RIGHT ABOVE AND BELOW On the Stones.

We used to have a barrow race, from here to Brighton with 6cwts. I'm not sure about the times, but Spitalfields did it in about 11½ hours, the Meat Market just under that and we smashed it. Six men took it in turns. I remember that Georgie Francis that trains Conteh today was one and also Johnny Francis but I don't know the others. They had a piano on the back of a motor and followed that. The Mayor was going to meet them in Brighton at nine in the morning but they got there at seven and so they fucked off home and left the Mayor. They smashed the records. Mind you, it's easy to pull a barrow that's full up.

There were parties at Christmas time, and nurses singing, and the police used to bring their Black Marias and fill them up with stuff and take it back to the hospitals for them. We'd take things over to Bow Street, stack it up, and supposition they'd come from Great Ormond Street, the police would take it back there . . . We used to have a terrific understanding with the police, and the local hospitals in case of emergencies. I went down to Charing Cross Hospital on a barrow once with a pulled stomach and they fixed me up right away.

There was about a dozen flower girls all round Charing Cross Station, but my mum, when she was a kid, sold flowers with her mum round Piccadilly Circus. It's right through the family. My mum was only a kid when she started, and her mum lived to be eighty-nine, and she didn't stop selling till she was eighty.

I was born in Drury Lane. I'm a proper old Covent Garden girl. I went to market with my dad at six or seven. I went to school there, and of a morning one or two of us would go round the market picking up the potatoes and the cabbage. The porters would say, 'Come 'ere, love, lift up your pinny', and chuck a couple in. Good old porters they were in them days. Then over there in Chandos Place there was a little poultry shop and we had to line up after school at 4.30 and run for all we was worth to get a place to pick up your threepenny worth of giblets. You'd get a bloody good wallop if you went home without your giblets. Sometimes I used to tell lies to the teacher. I'd say, 'Mum said could I leave at four o'clock instead of half past as she's not very well and I've got to go home and make her a cup of tea,' just so I could get to that shop. Saved me getting a good hiding.

As soon as we came out of school we had our tea and then we had to get to work. If my mother and father had a load of old duff violets we used to have to get inside a shop that didn't have too much light and holler out 'Penny a bunch, lovely violets!' Half dead, you know what I mean.

There was eleven of us. I'm the baby and I'm the only one left.

Bedford Chambers, by James Street,
now the Rock Garden restaurant.

On the Stones, at the north-west
corner of the Central Market.

On the east side of the
Central Market.

On South Row.

On the south side of the
Central Market.

There's only one way to have a market, and that's with chaos. Too ordered here. It's all done by numbers here. We always worked with a certain amount of confusion, in the old market, and that's why it was all right.

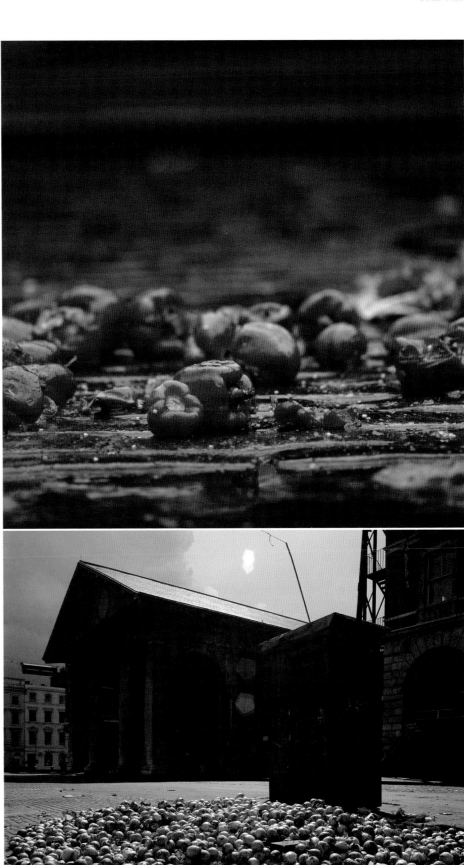

I can remember customers saying to me, 'What are you gonna do, Maggie, when you finish this game?' 'Don't talk to me, I wouldn't last two minutes,' I said. See, in the winter, it was rough, the wind over that Waterloo Bridge used to blow the flowers all over, tins of water and all. Passers-by used to help me pick 'em up, you know, and paper boys used to run up and I'd say, 'Isn't it all right, rotten bleeding wind!' But the winter is when you got a few bob, snowdrops, violets, primroses, anemones. They were our money-getters.

Spring, they knew that the daffs were coming in, in bud. Spring is coming, everybody bought in spring. We had to rough it in the bad weather but we earned a few bob. On Friday night I'd be out there years ago as they come from work, and they'd buy 'a bunch for me mum'. 'There's a good girl, buy your mum a bunch of flowers!' I used to say. but the last five or six years, you never heard those words, not for many a long day.

LEFT AND RIGHT The secondary article, or cotchel.

# ACKNOWLEDGMENTS

After nearly forty years I still feel a deep sense of gratitude to and for the people of the old market of Covent Garden. The passing of time has only strengthened my feeling of just how special that period of my life was. Yes, I know it was me who got out of bed at those ungodly hours of the morning, but it was *all* the people of the market who allowed me to work and hitch a ride on their lives in the closing years of Covent Garden Market in Covent Garden. I shall be forever grateful to have been given the privilege of knowing you a little.

Of course it is not possible to name all in the market who gave me continued help, assisting and co-operating in my efforts to capture that special something of the market. (Alas, so many have now passed on. I still thank them.) So please let it suffice to name but a few to represent the many: Derek S. Vinden, John Sullivan of Keeley's, Tommy Kennedy, Harold S. Tremain, Jack Tremain, George Rutledge, Harry Benstead, Fred Solomon, Jimmy Moore, John Bradman, Michael Walker, Peter Papa, Tony Gibbons, Mike Mole, Baron Werner, Ike and Lew Pyser, Rosie Bartlett, Bernie Holland, Les Green, Jimmy Mole, Jimmy Wheble, Ernie Hurley, Ron Clissold, Alex Bedford, Bert Hammond, Ray Lowe, Harry Chowles, Evelyn and Alfred Miknell, Conny Culwick, Terry O' Docherty, Bill Morritt, Pat Honey, Maggie Salter, Vic Fisk, Bernie Elliott, Bill Lodge, Johnny Watts, Denis Burrows, Alfie Marks and Jack Clark.

Special thanks to Chris Morris of the Flower Market, who has continued over the past thirty-eight years to let me make my little £10 or so wholesale flower purchase every week or two.

My thanks go also to the Covent Garden Market Authority and the Transport and General Workers' Union. Both were unfailing in their support for me.

Also from that time, special thanks must go to Dr Frances Kennett, who did the original transcribing from my tape-recorded interviews (my interview technique left much to be desired).

Very special thanks to Denis Bacon, photographer, friend and ex-boss, sadly no longer with us, who gave such support to my project by allowing me to work from his studio – and, more, his darkroom – for almost the whole of that period and after, rent-free, all in return for my being there when he needed help. Thank you Denis, God bless.

And to someone else who sadly is no longer with us, Sergeant Victor Martin, front of house Royal Opera, who was at times solely responsible for my being able to have a cultural life, after the whole day in the darkroom. Oh, those happy times standing in the stalls circle night after night, ballet after opera, opera after ballet.

For thirty-five years my colour work on the old market lay half-forgotten and totally undisturbed in a light-tight box which, for a short, horrifying while, became lost. It was my partner, Barbara Grant, who first started to push me to show her the colour work of Covent Garden. I must confess, the thought of digging all that lot up again did rather fill me with dread, and I asked myself 'Who the hell would be interested now?'

Well, not only Barbara but also a dear friend, Laurence Aston. I can really say that without these two this book simply would not have come into being. For it was Laurence who brought in the financial support of Frank Riess, another friend, enabling us to set up a company to manage the digitization of my Covent Garden archive. Laurence has done all the footwork to get this project off the ground; not a single aspect has he left unattended. Frank's advice and networking have also been invaluable.

Barbara not only convinced me in the beginning when I most needed it, but kept me on an even keel throughout the long editing process and corrected my English, while keeping the spirit of what I wanted to say. Her support for me never failed. Thank you, Barbara.

When Laurence told me that our book was to be published by Frances Lincoln I was thrilled, for I was already working with editor Jo Christian on the photographs for Rosemary Baird's book on *Goodwood*, published by Frances Lincoln in 2007. I was even more thrilled when I learned Jo was to be my editor on Covent Garden, and she has been such a support from minute one, always on hand for me.

As a grumpy old man, being introduced to the young designer Becky Clarke was a delight but also a bit of a shock. 'What on earth can *she* know about Covent Garden?' I asked myself. It was quite an odd feeling leaving my trannies with Becky to do the first layouts. A month later the grumpy old man went back to FL: was I over the moon when I saw the way Becky had put the pictures together. Thank you, Becky.

Thanks too to Tom Miller for bringing me into the twenty-first century. And to Professor Jack and Joyce Edelman for always being there for me.

Every effort has been made to trace those whose photographs appear in the book. We would be delighted to hear from anyone we have been unable to find.

Thank you all.

The Environs of COVENT GARDEN as recalled by the inhabitants

Peter McClure 1977

Scale

0    200 yards

150 metres